Microgreens:

A Beginner's Guide to the Benefits of Cultivation and Consumption

by Julia Winchester

Published by Cardigan River LLC

Copyright © Julia Winchester 2012

D0907809

Disclaimer

Table of Contents

Chapter 1: Introduction

Microgreens may be exactly what your diet needs. Fresh, organic greens like this are packed with nutrients difficult to find in such concentrations anywhere else. What are they? Why are so many people talking about them? If you haven't heard of them before, you soon will.

What Are Microgreens?

These tiny greens are definitely edible. They are simply a smaller form of the edible greens you are, or should be, eating and commonly find in your grocer's cooler. They come from the seeds of vegetables, herbs, as well as other plants. Most are not more than two inches in length, though they do have both stems and leaves.

What will you get from them? A simple bite into one and you will experience intense flavor, especially if the greens are organic. In other words, they taste great.

However, there is much more to microgreens than just this. As greens, they have a high level of beta-carotene in them. Though each variety has a different makeup, you can expect these to be nutrient-rich foods. As you will see, the health benefits of microgreens can be a big reason to grow them and eat them regularly.

Finding Great Microgreens

For those who would like to take advantage of all of the nutrients and great taste offered by microgreens, you have options. You can purchase them directly from suppliers. Most suppliers, though, work directly with restaurants. Some do offer options for direct buying, especially online.

On the other hand, why not grow them yourself? Requiring just a small amount of space, growing them yourself helps you ensure there is no risk of anything but organic elements present. Organically grown microgreens are the ideal choice.

Microgreens are not new. For many people, they are the ideal accompaniment to a recipe or the perfect choice for a green smoothie. Consider what these greens have to offer you.

How to Spot a Microgreen

There are many products on the market that claim to be unique greens and good-for-you foods. When it comes to finding microgreens, it is important to know the general specifications of these plants.

These plants are seedlings that have a stem that runs down the center. In most cases, when buying them, you will notice a cut at the base. This cut should occur just above the soil line when the microgreens are harvested. If it has the root or any seed component, this may not be a microgreen at all.

Generally, a quality product will have two fully developed leaves. For those looking for a very specific product, the highest quality, for example, there will usually be one pair of very small leaves. These leaves may not be fully developed.

Keep in mind that the term "microgreens" refers to a range of different plants. That means that each one is going to have some differences in the way they look. The size, number, and location of the leaves, for example, may be different. Here are some examples of what to look for when buying microgreens.

Microgreen basil is about 1 to 1 1/2 inches (2.5 to 3.7cm) in height. Across the very top, it should be about 1/2 to 1 inch (1.2 to 2.5cm) in width. This should include one set of small true leaves.

Microgreen borage is significantly different. It has a large plant. It measures one inch in height. Generally, it has a pair of larger cotyledon leaves at the top and no true leaves.

Microgreen mint, by comparison to either of these, is very small. The plant has very small cotyledon leaves and it will have between three and four sets of true leaves that measure about an inch (2.5cm) in height.

The key here is to look for smaller plants that provide a range of flavor options. Buying microgreens can be just what you need to spice up your dishes or plates. On the other hand, you may want to consider investing in growing them to sell them. The demand is significant!

Chapter 2: History of Microgreens

Haven't heard of microgreens previously? Most farmers call them seedlings. Of course, rabbits like to call them lunch. However, for everyday people, they are an ideal source of nutrients and a simple, effective way to dress up a plate.

In the United States, the production of microgreens began in the mid-1990s. Southern California, with its high temperatures and outstanding organic soils, was the ideal place to grow these plants.

Prior to the birth of microgreens, so to speak, the use of mesclun salad greens was a popular focus for growers. This is the practice of growing greens specifically meant to be put into a salad together. Farmers began growing mesclun salad greens in the 1980s. However, microgreens are an even newer
variety. In fact, they are grown and then harvested at a younger stage than most other types of greens. Though they differ significantly from sprouts, these young plants are still rather new to the culinary table.

The initial reason for creating these greens was to provide a garnish for restaurant dishes. Even today, it is very common to find them adorning your dinner plate at a higher-priced establishment. Though this is one of the most common uses for them, many everyday people enjoy both the flavor and the nutritional value of these greens.

As a result, the popularity of the greens has skyrocketed. Today, people want them sent directly to their homes. They crave the flavor and, more importantly, want the access to nutrition.

They Are Not Really New

The fact is, microgreens are just the start of plants. Farmers plant seeds and water them. The plants grow. The difference here is when the farmer picks them. Microgreens are grown to a significantly shorter stature, so to speak. Yet, they have always been around. Now is it your turn to get them into your diet and your greenhouse, but even the windowsill in the kitchen will likely do well.

Today, you will find a mix of microgreens available. In fact, they are grown throughout the country. The most common options include arugula, kale, cilantro, beets and basil.

In addition, some producers create a mixture of these and sell it as a "rainbow mix." The bottom line here is that these greens are readily available to you and new varieties continue to become even more readily available. You can, grow your own, too of course.

Chapter 3: Sprouts Versus Microgreens

One of the biggest question people want to have an answer to is the difference between sprouts and microgreens. Sprouts are one of the most common types of nutrient rich foods available today. Many consumers seek them out because of the numerous health claims about them, including things such as the ability of these sprouts to provide a super dose of nutrition in a small size.

It is important to know that sprouts are not the same thing as microgreens. This is a common misconception. In fact, some of the informational pieces you find online may even interchange these two terms. Yet, a few specific things you need to know differentiate the two. The best way to see this is to compare the differences in production of these two nutrient-rich food sources.

What Are Sprouts?

Sprouts start like any other plant does. They come from germinated seeds. When a person consumes sprouts, he or she is consuming the seed, the root, the pale and stem as well as the under developed leaves of the plant. Microgreens are significantly different, as you will see.

Sprouts are grown nearly entirely in water. In other words, there is no dirt or soil involved. The seeds are not specifically planted like they are with other plants. To grow sprouts, the user must plant the seed (usually at a very high density) in the specific enclosed containers designed for sprouting. The seed will then germinate. This process happens quickly because the moisture level is so high. The humidity even encourages the growth to happen at a much faster rate than what happens with traditional plant growth.

Another option for the growth of seeds is in cloth bags. These bags are dipped in water regularly. This again keeps the moisture level very high and encourages the rapid growth of the seeds.

One of the more common ways sprouts are grown, though, is in a rotating drum. The seeds are first soaked so that they absorb as much of the moisture as they can. Then, they are placed into the drum that rotates regularly. Sometimes, they are just placed into a container. In all situations, the humidity is very high, sometimes as high as 100 percent. The temperature is maintained around 80 degrees Fahrenheit (26 degrees Celsius) as well.

This process takes about 48 hours. At the completion of it, the seeds are sprouts and, as such, they are then packed up and sold on the market.

Usually, this process will occur in the dark or in very low light situations. This also contributes to the rapid growth of the seeds. It may seem like this is everything you've heard not to do when trying to grow seeds in a garden or a flower pot, but when the goal is to rapidly grow sprouts, this method works well.

After Being Sold

Once the seeds are sold, they are not ready for consumption just yet. Rather, it will take a process of soaking and rinsing the seeds to get them ready to eat. Sometimes this can amount to two to six times a day. This process helps to prevent any spoilage from occurring.

Of course, no leaves have grown more than just little buds in this entire time. All you will see is the very little seed with the actual stem-like coming from it. The leaves, if any, are very small and insignificant.

When you buy sprouts like this on the market, you can expect them to be a tangled mass of pale roots. They are not single plants sold as such. Rather, they are usually purchased as a mass of mesh.

How and Why Microgreens Are Different

If you tried to grow microgreens in any of these environments, they would not grow. The significant difference in these two types of growth methods for seeds is what makes the result (the nutrients and the flavor) do different between sprouts and microgreens.

Microgreens require a different environment. Consider the differences in how these plants grow.

Rather than soaking in water,, they need soil or some type of soil substitute. For example, they can be grown in peat moss.

Rather than lurking in the dark, microgreens need light. Often, the light levels need to be somewhat intense.

In addition, humidity is not meant to be very high when growing microgreens. They do not do well in that environment. Rather, they need air circulation that's warm and regularly filtered.

When you compare the density of the number of seeds planted at one time, microgreens are a small number comparatively. This limited number allows the plant to grow in the soil separated from the other plants growing with it. The goal here is not to stop the growth of the plant, but rather to allow it to grow in the right manner.

Additionally, microgreens need more time. They do not go from seed to sprout in just two days. Rather, they take one to two weeks to grow. In some cases, depending on the circumstances and seed types, it can take up to six weeks to get to the right maturity level.

Microgreens do have leaves when you purchase them. In most cases, the leaves must fully expand prior to the time that the plant is harvested for sale or use.

Yet another difference in that microgreens are sold in containers in which they are still growing. Rather than a mess of sprouts, microgreens actually still have the ability to grow because they are still anchored in the soil. This means that the person who plants to use them cuts them right at the peak time.

How You Can Tell the Difference

If you are planning to make a purchase of microgreens but do not want to end up with sprouts, you'll want to look for a few telltale signs. First, if you purchase something that looks like a stem and the roots are not included, this is a microgreen. If the plant was grown in water only, it will likely be sold as the entire patch of seeds, roots, stem, and buds.

Another good indication is the level of growth found. Sprouts have very little development and they have very little actual production of leaves. Rather, when buying microgreens, you will see more of the leafy development occurring.

It is also a good idea to look at the color. If the color is less than vibrant green, chances are good you have a sprout or you have a plant grown under artificial light. This may also limit the actual flavor of the plant as a result.

Why You Need to Know the Difference

Although there is a flavor difference and there may be a significant health difference in these two types of plants, most people do not realize the difference. However, it can be important to know not only what you are buying but also whom you are buying it from.

In 2011, the US Food and Drug Administration ("FDA") announced that 52 people died and thousands more were sick because of consuming organic sprouts. This occurred in Europe, not the United States. In the US, the FDA has sought to regulate that any production of sprouts is better regulated.

The European Union Food Safety Authority has also put in place warnings to consumers. They warned that consumers should not consume sprouts or sprouted seeds unless they cook them thoroughly. This is not always a good thing especially since this reduces the flavor, texture, and nutrient level.

Sprout outbreaks can include some very dangerous pathogens. Specifically, E coli and salmonella have both been found in these plants as the cause of the outbreaks.

The FDA has put in place various guidelines for the production of these sprouts in an effort to minimize the amount of risk for any type of outbreak. This process helps to reduce the production of bacteria. By reducing the presence of the bacteria, it is possible to reduce the risk of any food borne illness from developing.

9

The problem is the process in which sprouts are created - the high humidity and low light levels - actually makes it very difficult for sprouts to grow without any presence of bacteria. This is why so many restaurants and grocers have pulled the product from the market and use. It is just too much of a risk.

Buying the Right Product

Keep in mind that the FDA now has specific guidelines in place to ensure that buyers can purchase the right type of product. Microgreens and sprouts are very different and any product that is being sold as a microgreen should not use the words "sprouts" or "sprouting."

For those who wish to grow and sell microgreens, it is very important to know the difference and to provide the proper labeling. If an FDA inspection were to happen, you may find that not all inspectors know the difference.

In other words, if you plan to buy or sell microgreens, you need to ensure what you are after is a true microgreen and not a sprout. The difference could mean the difference between health and illness - not to mention a poor taste!

For additional information, please see the FoodSafety.gov links in Chapter 9: Additional Resources.

Chapter 4: The Health Benefits of Consuming Microgreens

Although microgreens were originally developed as a way to garnish plates, they do have significant health benefits to them. For those who are looking for a way to create a tasty meal, adding a few of these on your plate may be just what you need.

Let us be honest and upfront about the health benefits of microgreens. It is important to know exactly what you are eating and to realize that these plants may not be the super food you thought they were.

In short, there have been no studies done on microgreens. There has been a lot of hype about them. In some cases, there have been reports that microgreens are somehow a super food that can change your life, help you to drop weight quickly or otherwise to enhance your health.

Keep in mind, there are no scientific studies behind these reports. In other words, it is critical for you to make realistic estimations of the health benefits of these plants. Here are a few things to keep in mind.

Microgreens are a healthy food. They do contain nutrition and it is likely similar to that which is in the larger varieties of the plant. They are not bad for you unless you have an allergy to it.

The US Department of Agriculture has not done a nutritional analysis of microgreens. Keeping this in mind, it is important to note that there is no specific indication of how much of what vitamin or nutrient is included.

There are numerous varieties of microgreens. As a direct result, there is no way to tell you what is in all microgreens. Consider the individual plants and their likely nutritional level.

In some cases, it may be possible that younger plants, like microgreens, have less nutrient value than the mature plant.

What About Sprouts, Though?

You may be wondering why nutrition is not as readily available for microgreens as it is for sprouts. There have been many claims about sprouts, too. Sprouts, which we have noted are not the same, often contain a high level of Sulphoraphane Glucosinolate (SGS) in them. This is a nutrient commonly found in the seed. Since you eat the seed with the sprout, it makes sense that this nutrient would be included. However, you will get a higher level of this nutrient if you ate the seed prior to its growing into a sprout!

As a point of reference, it is also important to point to the USDA's opinion related to sprouts. According to the organizations, sprouts suggest a promising role in promoting health. However, no research is present to provide any specific conclusion to this point. It does not specifically mention microgreens, though.

What Does This Mean to You?

If you wanted to purchase and begin using microgreens for health benefits, do so. It is likely that these plants do contain numerous health benefits because they are made up of the same components, and they are grown in the same way or a better way, than their more mature varieties.

Should you base your diet on the consumption of microgreens? The answer to that is no. You will need to consume other foods, too. However, it does mean that you can add them to your diet as a healthy option. Stay away from sprouts and invest in microgreens instead. You will get nutritional value in a positive way
through these products.

At the same time, be mindful that other companies and organizations are often promoting a range of claims about the super food qualities of microgreens. Ask for the research to verify this before you count on it for your own benefit.

There is no reason not to throw them into a dish or to a drink. Doing so is likely to give you a nutrition boost.

Throughout this book, we have included areas of information about specific health benefits related to specific types of microgreens. Remember, each type has different vitamins and nutrients in it. The information provided is specific to the type grown.

Chapter 5: Popular Types of Microgreens

No matter why you want to enjoy them, there are some great varieties of microgreens available. What you should know, though, is that microgreens come in all shapes and sizes. In addition, know that the flavor of each is different. It is often not as strong as the mature variety of the plant. However, it does offer a nice pop of flavor and freshness in most varieties.

Keep in mind that the seeds used to grow microgreens are the same seeds that are found in full sized herbs, leafy greens, and vegetables. These are just harvested earlier than other varieties.

Consider the following as popular options just right for most needs:

Arugula

Arugula, a popular lettuce used in salads, has a peppery, mild bite to it. It adds a nice punch of flavor in the microgreen size. If you are buying this plant to grow on your own, here is what you need to know:

- It does grow faster than most types.

- You can find it in an organically grown variety.

- In terms of health benefits, arugula, in its full-grown size, has a high level of antioxidants in it.

- Use it in smoothies, cooked recipes including stews and in salads.

Beets

You know the health benefits of eating beets - your mother probably made you eat them when you were younger. Micro beets, often called micro beet tops, have long, red stems and green, oblong shaped leaves.

- A great option for using in salads for their color.

- They add a beautiful addition to a holiday dish.

- The flavor is subtle and not overpowering in any way.

- A softer beet flavor is common with beet top microgreens.

Broccoli

A popular microgreen is broccoli. It has a milder taste than that of fully-grown broccoli but you can still tell they are in the same family. Consider the following:

- Broccoli has a high level of heart-disease fighting antioxidants in it.

- Look for, and buy only, organic. Grow your own organically.

- Use in salads, as a garnish or in a smoothie for a subtle but tasty flavor boost.

- These microgreens grow at a moderate rate.

Cucumber

Microgreens from cucumbers are fresh and light. They make a great addition to any meal when you want a soft addition of flavor.

- Look for light green leaves that are smooth to be sure they are microgreens if buying harvested varieties.

- Add to protein dishes or to add flavor to basic fish.

- The flavor is succulent and still tastes significantly like cucumbers.

Cabbage

For those that enjoy cabbage dishes, you will find both red and green cabbage microgreens readily available. Choose these for a mild flavor or, in the case of red cabbage, a nice pop of color.

- Tender greens have a mild flavor.

- You can grow them easily - a simple microgreen to grow that is relatively resistant to disease.

- A good choice for overall health considering fully-grown cabbage is a good source of vitamins and other nutrients.

Celery

Celery greens are a good option because of their mild flavor and overall appealing taste. This is a popular option. Some companies sell mixed celery greens with other types of microgreens included. However, you can grow them on your own as well.

- This is a slow grower. It will take more time than most microgreens to reach maturity, for microgreens, but it is well worth it.

- They are small and they remain small. You will want to harvest them at just a few inches.

- It can be hard to find quality seeds, especially organic varieties.

- This is a good aromatic addition to your microgreen garden. The sweet smell will lure you back every day.

Chia

A popular mature plant, chia is also available as a microgreen. This variety can be a very good option for those who want a simple and nutritious addition to their smoothies.

- Chia, when sold as a fully-grown plant, has a rich source of nutrients, including antioxidants.

- Look for certified organic products for the best pop of flavor.

- The flavor is subtle but worth investing in.

- This plant is not difficult to grow and takes a moderate length of time.

- The black and white coloring makes it a stand out in any garden space or on any plate.

Flax

Flax is normally sold as a seed or in ground up form. However, it is also possible to purchase flax microgreens and get the same or a similar, taste. This makes a great addition to a salad or a smoothie.

- You can find both brown and golden flax options.

- Flax, in its fully-grown variety, has a number of health benefits, including a natural dietary aid benefit and heart-health benefits.

Kale

Kale is a nutritious, easy to enjoy leafy green vegetable. Kale has a vibrant green color. As a microgreen, you can expect to enjoy these in salads, as a garnish or just about any way you want to.

- The seeds, even organic varieties, are inexpensive and rather easy to find.

- It produces white stemmed plants that have green leaves.

- This is a faster grower, but not so fast that it is hard to manage.

- You may find both green and a red variety, both available in organic forms.

- The mild flavor makes it easy to put into virtually anything you hope to enjoy.

Mizuna

You will find mizuna to be in the same family as bok choy and other types of Asian vegetables including broccoli rabe and Chinese cabbage.

- This is a fast growing microgreen.

- Chefs love to add them because of their beauty and their flavor.

- Still new and somewhat unknown in the culinary world, mizuna is a great pop when you want something that people will ask, "what's that?"

- The flavor is milder but similar to tatsoi.

- Add it to a mesclun mix for the best overall results in a dish.

Pea Tendrils

Another type of microgreen to try is pea tendrils. These are microgreens stemming from the production of peas. If you have ever grown peas before, you know these are long, vine-like plants that spread out virtually everywhere. The tendrils are the small shots that come out of the vine and coil around the various fences or other structures to provide support for the climbing vine. These are a fantastic type of microgreen.

- They are delicate in flavor and yet a beautiful addition to a plate.

- They taste like fresh peas, right off the vine, perhaps even a bit spring-like in their fresh taste.

- They are often sold in a mixture of lengths, usually about three to four inches in length. They will also have about a dozen leaves on them and a few tendrils (this is the curling portion.)

- They make a nice statement on a plate, often a dramatic display of greenery on the plate.

Peppercress

This microgreen is a great choice for all around flavor. What you will find is that the flavors of peppercress are complex and biting. It has a nice peppery blend that is perfect for virtually any dish where you want something with a tart flavor.

- Lots of flavor but in a microgreen size.

- Put it in a mix, rather than a standalone on a plate. A little goes a long way with the bolder flavor.

- A long and skinny microgreen, it is beautiful too.

Red Cabbage

Red cabbage microgreens are an excellent overall choice. They are beautiful microgreens and add a sense of class to any dish. They have a beautiful red coloring to them in the leaf, which is unlike most other microgreens. More so, the stem is a softer, almost pink colored stem. This definitely makes a beautiful impression on a plate.

- You can add a good number of these to a plate for a flavor additive.

- It does have a nice taste and texture but it is not an overpowering taste. This allows it to blend well with soft foods including fish.

- It does not taste much like cabbage and your guests are unlikely to know that is what it is.

- It is tender and easy to eat, too.

Red Mustard

For another red variety of microgreens consider red mustard. This does taste like mustard but like most types of microgreens, the taste is not as strong or as tart. That is often a great thing in this type of dish.

- It has a natural flavor similar to that of soft Dijon mustard.

- Adding this microgreen to a salad is like adding a touch of mustard to your dressing except you do not have to blend it.

- It is a good choice for those who want to add a bit of something different to a salad mix.

- For meats, denser vegetable dishes or even fragrant salads, add this microgreen alongside red cabbage for an interesting and pleasing taste.

- You will know it is red mustard microgreens by the leaves. They are heart shaped and have a darker red coloring. The stems of the plants are green. The leaves have a beautiful red coloring throughout them.

Red Kale

Also known as, red Russian kale, this microgreen is a good choice. Even if you would not normally eat kale in your salad without cooking it first, this microgreen gives you the ability to do that with its better flavor.

- This microgreen has a soft, easy to enjoy flavor to it.

- There is a touch of sweetness present here, which makes it a good option for vegetables.

- Use it within your salad mixes for good results but you will be able to add it to the dinner plate as a beautiful garnish, too.

Tatsoi

Microgreen tatsoi is becoming a more popular option. Chances are good you've seen it before even though you may not have known about it.

- Often locally grown and served on tables of chefs who want something a bit more original to garnish their plates.

- Sometimes it is known as a spinach mustard microgreen. It may also be called rosette bok choy or spoon mustard.

- The taste is unique. It is a mixture of a subtle bok choy along with a slight hint of mustard.

- You'll find it has just two small leaves on the green stem. Sometimes, it looks like a two-leafed clover.

- A nice addition to a dish as a garnish, but you can also add it into a salad mix if you would like it to play more of a role in the dish.

These are some of the most common forms of microgreens. Keep in mind, though, that any vegetable plant can start out as a microgreen and most are definitely worth enjoying. You may simply want to try to grow your own plant in this form if you would like to do so.

Chapter 6: Supplies for Growing Your Own

Let's face it, there is nothing more enjoyable than eating some freshly grown plants. That is, except for enjoying those you have grown yourself. Many people, including many chefs, enjoy microgreens but do not want to pay the hefty price tag for buying and shipping them home or to their location. The fact is, for microgreens to taste great, they need to be fresh. However, that is often hard to do when you are buying from a company that may be located in another part of the country.

Instead of trying to fight the process, why not try to grow your own? You will find that growing microgreens is a very easy process, especially with the right tools in your hand to do so. Consider the following before you get started:

Dedicated Space

The first thing you need before you even get started with microgreens is the space to grow them. Keep in mind that most take between one and six weeks to reach their peak stage for harvesting. However, you can create a cycle so that you are consistently harvesting what you need for dishes and still have new microgreens growing.

To do this, though, you need to have enough space for the process. You will want to dedicate space near natural light, if possible. Remember, these are not sprouts and they do need low humidity conditions with plenty of light. You can invest in growing lights if you would like to speed up or better regulate the process. Still, create a large enough space for the number of plants you plan to grow.

Select a tabletop - these plants are not going to grow for a long time. This means that they will not get very large and will not be very heavy. However, if you plan to grow a large number of them, you will need more room and a sturdy table!

Keep in mind that you do not have to grow them indoors. It can be easier to do so because it minimizes the risk that animals will munch on them. Additionally, it is easier to control the humidity indoors than it is outdoors. Still, these plants are mostly easy to grow anywhere.

Dedicate Time

Time is another component to the process. In order to get enough growing out of your microgreens, it is a good idea to plan to spend some time with the plants. Most of the time, it is necessary to spend a few minutes every few days taking care of them. Most do not need a lot of attention dedicated to them - they do like to grow well on their own, as long as you provide the medium to allow that to happen.

Nevertheless, just keeping the process of growing and harvesting going, you will need to dedicate some time to the process. You can minimize this time by using organic soils that hold water well so that you do not have to spend as much time watering them.

If you are planning to grow and use microgreens in your restaurant's dishes, you will need to dedicate far more time to the process. Of course, if this is a large-scale operation, you will likely hire someone to help you with the process!

It is also important to put some time and effort into learning how to grow microgreens well. Anyone can purchase seeds, sprinkle them in place, and wait for the sprouts and greens to begin growing. However, to get the best possible results, you do need to put more effort into the process. Here are some things to keep in mind:

- For the best results, buy organic seeds. You do not want to start with something that is already contaminated with various pesticides.

- Look for a quality provider of materials. It is imperative that you trust your supply, otherwise you could invest a lot of time and money into the process without a lot of result.

- Always use organic products. This includes your soils. This is one of the best ways to reduce the risk of eating something that is not as good for you as it could be.

- Additionally, it is a good idea to keep working to perfect the process. This means learning from mistakes and giving it another chance if the first round does not go the way you want it to.

Growing Indoors

If you plan to grow microgreens indoors, you'll need the space to do so. Then, you'll need to assemble the following resources for the job:

Seeds

The good news is that seeds are easy to find and easy to use. You do not have to buy anything strange here. Rather, you just need to buy the same seeds you would if you were planting a garden in the backyard. You can find a variety of microgreen-specific seed products on the market, though. Here are some things to keep in mind with these products:

- Buy organic. It can be hard to tell but any product that is truly organic will be labeled as that.

- Buy quality. You will find that buying in-season is the best possible way to get a healthy growth. In other words, avoid using seeds from several years ago.

- You can buy and use whatever type you like. This includes heirlooms, though without producing the fruits and vegetables these may be a tad more expensive than it is worth!

- Keep in mind that storing your seeds is also important. Keep them in a dry location without sunlight prior to growing them.

Then there is the thought of buying mixes. There are many organic microgreen mixes being sold. You may even find that you can buy the grown microgreens in these mixes. As long as you like each of the ingredients within them, you will find this is a good idea. On the other hand, if you are using just a few springs on plates and want a uniform result, go with a single variety. Mixes do not guarantee a good flavor combination either.

Trays

You will want to use trays, plastic or recyclable material are fine, to hold your soil and your seeds. When buying these, be sure you look for those that have drain holes throughout the bottom. They should also have ridges to encourage water to flow out of them. Choose trays that are about a foot or so wide so they are easy to move around, as you need to. Some are significantly larger. That is fine to use as long as they are durable enough for you easily to move them.

Look for those that are sturdy and durable as well. You can reuse these repeatedly if you buy a quality product rather than very thin plastics.

Soils

There are many schools of thought on what type of soil to use. There are a few things to remember before you start to buy these.

Always go with organic product. Do not buy anything that is not 100 percent organic. It will be easy to taste and feel the difference in the finished microgreens.

Look for a combination of organic material in the soil. All microgreens need food from the soil, but this comes from the compost included. It is best to choose soils that are composts made of only vegetation matter.

Loosely packed soil is best. Sometimes, you will find moisture-holding materials. This is okay as long as it is organic and does not create a soggy soil for the plants to grow in.

If you plan to use soil from out of your garden, be sure it is not too heavily clay based. You need the nutrition that comes from lighter mixes. In addition, the roots need to grow easily into the soil. You never want to pack it into place too tightly.

Spray Bottles

It is a good idea to pick up a spray bottle to use for watering. Because of how tiny the stems are, pouring water from a pitcher into the tray is not going to work well. This could cause the seeds to wash right away. Instead, focus on a spray bottle with a misting feature.

Other Items

You will find a wide range of products on the market that can be a good choice or they may not be worth your time. For example, one of the key elements of growing a large amount of microgreens on a consistent basis is the use of a pH balanced soil. You can purchase various kits to test the soil with, if you would like to do so.

You can also find additives that can be put into the soil if the composition of it is not balanced properly. These are okay to use as long, as they are organic in nature, and do not contain any type of chemicals.

You will find other products available as well including testing strips, various nutrient additives, and hydroponic growing systems. If you would like to invest in these do so, but realize that you do not need much more than what has already been presented.

Growing Outdoors

You do have the option of growing microgreens outdoors. Many people do this and, naturally, this is likely to work well. Though you will have to manage the climate and animals better, this is a good way to get that natural flavor of strong, young plants. There is something more enjoyable about growing them in direct sunlight in the natural ground.

You will still need all of the resources included above. Additionally, you may want to think about a few addition things:

Create a garden bed or raised bed for the best possible results. This will elevate your workspace while also providing easier access to the microgreens as they are growing.

You will need to manage pests well. Though many people would instinctively grab a pesticide to do this, do not do it. You are contaminating your microgreens by doing so. Rather, use natural alternatives. This is one of the hardest challenges for microgreen growers working outside since the plants will not have a long lifetime to overcome any initial damage.

Larger pests, including deer and other animals are known for munching on microgreens. These are a favorite among many of these animals. Using fencing can help but ensure it is small enough to prevent any access from the smaller critters in your area.

Be sure there is excellent drainage. You do not want the soil to be saturated and to stay that way after a rain. This can lead to bacteria growth that can be detrimental to the plants themselves. If you are able to pick a location, choose a slope that allows water naturally to drain away.

Just like any other material, your soil needs to be organic. This may mean starting with something brand new rather than using what you already have in place. Be sure to choose organic soils because of the nutrients included and the lack of pesticides. If you are growing on a large scale, you may want to choose to buy in bulk.

Containers Work, Too

If you want a good combination of growing outdoors but also in a movable tray, then use containers outdoors. This is a great overall solution because it will minimize many of your risks from pests and climate control issues. You can always bring it in if you do not want to risk a frost or a bad storm.

Container gardening for microgreens is a fantastic choice. Use the same materials as you would for traditional tray growing of microgreens.

You can find virtually all of the supplies you need for microgreen growing online. The process of buying them is easy enough, but you do not have to spend a lot of money on them. It is better to invest in seed quality than in tray quality if you have to make a choice.

Now that you know what to buy, the next step is making the microgreen magic happen.

Chapter 7: How to Grow Microgreens

You have already learned the basics of how to grow microgreens just by reading the supply chapter. There are a few more things you need to plan for when it comes to growing these wonderful plants.

It's Not Hard

A good thing to know about growing microgreens is that most plants are easy to grow. Unless you select a type of plant that is not an easy grower, and most seed providers will tell you this, you will find that the overall process is easier than you think.

However, you do have to be consistent with care. Be sure you have a solid understanding of what each plant variety needs. Most plants started with seeds require the same basic structure in the first days. Here are a few things you need to know.

Every type of seed you purchase should come with specific instructions on how to grow them. The key here is to realize that plants are all different and that means everything from the temperature to soil type can be vastly different from one type of plant to the next.

Most seeds require the same growing conditions. This means that you can often grow seeds together. However, with microgreens, you will likely grow the plants in the same containers that you harvest them - there is no transplantation necessary because the plants grow only to a certain point before you need to harvest them.

Keep seed types separate for best care and growing. This will help to ensure you can harvest plants at the same time. If you do plan to mix, buy a mixture of seeds designed to grow evenly together or select varieties that have the same germination period.

With this in mind, you are ready to start growing your own seeds. The following steps make the process easier for you to do than you may realize.

Planting Seeds

When you are ready to plant seeds, and you can plant at any time of the year and create your own growing pattern, the first step is to ensure all items are clean and sanitized. This includes any growing trays you are reusing.

You will want to fill the growing trays with your soil mixture. If you are buying soil be sure to mix in compost that's all organic and vegetation to ensure there is enough food for your plants to grow from.

Do not pack the soil in tightly. You want the seeds to be able to germinate and easily grow the roots outward.

Scatter your seeds within the tray. If you are using individual "pods" as your growing tray, you can usually put one or two in these. However, it is not necessary to use these. An open tray is often a good option.

Plant the seeds about 1/8 to 1/4 of an inch (0.3 to 0.6cm) apart. They do need some room but not nearly what they require when they are fully grown plants. Seed packages often state the amount of room that these seeds need when the plants are growing to a much larger size. Just a few inches is all that's needed even for larger plants.

Add about 1/2 inch (1.2cm) of soil over the top of the seeds. You do not want to pack this down, but you do want the seeds covered in the soil medium.

Water well initially. You do not want the soil to ever fully dry out. However, it should not be super wet either. Keep it damp and using a spray bottle to water the plants rather than anything that is going to disrupt the flow of the soil.

Place the trays in an area where there is at least four hours of sun each day. It is best to get at least that but there is no limit to how much they can get. If you place them by a window with air circulating, ensure the soil does not dry out.

If you are planting outdoors, follow the same steps. but this time plant them directly into the flower bed. You will also need to monitor for any weed growth. Remove these plants right away. You do not want anything growing in the trays or outdoors between your microgreens - this will disrupt their ability to grow well.

To Fertilize or Not To

The fact is that there is usually no reason to add any fertilizer to your microgreens. The reason for this is again because you will be removing the plants well before they become large enough to require additional nutrients that the soil is not able to provide.

However, if you are not starting with a quality soil mixture, adding organic matter to the soil is a good idea. In fact, you can do this in between your harvesting and seeding for the next round. Only add organic material to the mix.

In the outdoors, it is easier to add more organic material to the soil. However, do not disturb the growing seeds to do so. This will not benefit the plant. It is also a good idea to avoid any fertilizers that add to the soil through misting or through sprinklers. This is often too much water to add at one time and it will have little benefit on your microgreens - they really do not need much fertilizer to get these results.

Harvesting your Microgreens

As your seeds grow, you will not have to do much with them. In fact, the process only takes a matter of time. You will want to monitor for sunlight, dampness, and any weeds. You do not need to do any type of soil digging or mulching. This is not necessary and it is best to allow the seeds simply to grow.

As we have mentioned, microgreens are not just a stem and roots - those are sprouts. Microgreens grow a bit larger. The best time to harvest them is when they get their true leaves. True leaves are the first leaves that the plants develop. You will want these to grow until they are several inches in length (including the stem of the plant.) For most plant seeds, this process takes between 10 and 14 days, but it can take longer in some situations. You will need simply to monitor them until they reach about three to four inches in length from the ground up.

When they get this large, the next step is to snip them. In other words, you do not want just to pull them out. Rather, use a sharp pair of scissors to cut them right above the dirt line. Most microgreens do not have any included roots or seeds in them. Sometimes, growers will send them this way, though, to ensure the plants live through the shipping process.

After this point, though, there is nothing to expect from the seeds. They have done their work and there is not much more that can be done. Since the seeds have used their stored energy to grow to this point, they cannot grow any further. You have snipped away the leaves, which would otherwise continue to help the plant to grow. There is no way for these seeds to generate any new growth.

Therefore, if you would like to do so, you can begin a new crop at this point. In doing so, you will just need to rotate the soil a bit and then add new seeds. If you plan to add any fertilizer in, now is a good time to do so. You will then be able to add another layer of seeds and start the process over again. You do not even need to remove any roots from the old plants - that is a fantastic source of organic material for the new seeds to use for growth.

Chapter 8: Uses and Recipes for Microgreens

Having these beautiful, fresh plants from your garden, it is now time to use them. These are so easy to use and you cannot go wrong. In fact, if you want to, you can just pick one and start enjoying it. Eating them raw is just fine. However, if you are interested in a few other uses for them, aside from a beautiful garnish on top of your dinner plate, consider the following tips and ideas:

Salad Greens

One of the most common ways to use microgreens is as a mix into any of your salads. They work well in virtually all situations. In the previous chapters, we have given you some examples of great greens to try as well as what they taste like. All you need to do is to choose those that you enjoy the most and add them to your salad.

They work well with most types of salads, including fresh spring mixes. You will want to ensure that the plants are added based on their flavor composition not just the way they look. Some are bitter while others have a nice peppery bite that adds a lot of character to an otherwise boring salad.

Smoothies

For those who want to extract the healthy goodness that comes from these plants, a great solution for doing so is in a smoothie. For this, you can mix them in with other green vegetables or you can add them in on their own. Here are some ideas.

Mix some microgreens of your choosing with spinach, coconut milk and ice for a cool, refreshing green smoothie packed with nutrition. Use about a cup (¼ liter) of each ingredient.

You can mix them with fruits as well. By mixing them with fruits, you get a sweet smoothie that tastes great but has the nutrition of a green vegetable drink. Kids will love this.

You can use microgreens alone with just some ice and a splash of lemon and then add in your favorite adult beverage to make a frozen cocktail. This is definitely something your guests will not expect.

Use microgreens as you would other types of greens in these drinks. You can find thousands of smoothie recipes on the Internet to give you this amount of flexibility.

As a Topping

Another way to get the most out of these goodies is to use it as a topping. Do you run a burger restaurant and want to offer something different to your guests? A good way to do just that is to top your favorite burgers with a few springs of microgreens. Do this in place of or alongside the use of lettuce. You can do this at home, too.

You can use microgreens to top off a vegetable medley. For example, roast your favorite vegetables together with a bit of olive oil. After they are done but still warm, toss in some chopped microgreens. This adds a wow factor and it will give the vegetables a fresh taste.

You can use them as a topping for your favorite soaps and stews in the same way. Add them to any type of cooked food for a burst of fresh flavor.

Even More Ways to Use Them

Are you looking for a few new ways to use microgreens? Take a taste of the following options:

- Add them as a garnish on top of prepared eggs - anyway you like them.

- Create a specialized, microgreen salad with nothing more than the greens you enjoy. You will not need any dressing here.

- Top fish with them before or after you broil it.

- Right out of the oven, the addition of microgreens on top of a white fish or on top of chicken breast can give this otherwise boring food some beauty.

- Chop them and mix them into rice blends for something unique and flavorful.

- Put them in any of your favorite savory drinks, including those that have alcohol in them. They make a great addition to Bloody Marys, martinis, or tonics.

- Want to create a grown-up shake. Make a favorite shake flavor and then top the creamy ice cream with a bit of alcohol and blend. Top with a spring or two of a fresh microgreen for added flavor and a beautiful touch.

- Add them to pizzas for something different and unique.

The fact is, you can use microgreens for a wide variety of options. Use them for any type of dish you hope to create when you want to add a fresh flavor. On the other hand, you can just much on them all day long. They work just like mint and other fresh herbs. You can use them interchangeably as such in all of your favorite dishes.

There's no doubt you will find a wide range of great ways to add flavor and beauty to your dishes with the use of microgreens. It has never been easier to do so, in fact!

Chapter 9: Additional Resources

Growing microgreens is a process. It starts with getting together the commitment to put time into the process. Once you take this time, though, you will find it is easier for you to enjoy microgreens any time you would like to do so.

There are some great resources available to help you in your quest to growing microgreens or just using them. The following are some of our favorite resources.

Books to Further Your Education

There are many varieties and types of microgreens available. Check out these books for more details and added information.

"Microgreens: A Guide to Growing Nutrient-Packed Greens," written by Eric Franks and Jasmine Richardson - This book's easy to read style is a great asset. If you want to learn more in-depth methods for growing these plants this guide provides you with that amount of help.

"Microgreens: How to Grow Nature's Own Superfood," written by Fionna Hill – This book is a good resource to have on hand especially if you plan to grow microgreens as a way to improve your health. Remember the science is not fully there yet, but this book offers some great insight into the process.

"Wheatgrass, Sprouts, Microgreens and the Living Food Diet," written by K. K. Fowlkes - This book provides more information than just microgreens. We love the microgreens information included, but for those who want to really amplify their diet and get more nutrition into place, a combination of these great nutrient-rich foods is a good choice. We suggest focusing on microgreens first.

"Indoor Gardening the Organic Way: How to Create a Natural and Sustaining Environment for Your Houseplants", written by Julie Bawden-Davis - This book is great not necessarily for microgreen information, but rather for the organic-specific information for indoor growers. You really do want to keep your plants organic and this guide will help you to do just that.

FoodSafety.gov Press Releases and Blog Postings

Sprouts: What You Should Know -
http://www.foodsafety.gov/keep/types/fruits/sprouts.html

Hold the Raw Sprouts, Please -
http://www.foodsafety.gov/blog/raw_sprouts.html

Supplies and More

When it comes to growing microgreens, you really do want to have access to the best seeds and supplies. You will find a wide range of sources available to help you with these needs. However, the following are some of our favorites because they provide such a fantastic wealth of options for new growers to get started with in growing microgreens right at home, or even in the back lot of your restaurant if that's what your goal is!

FreshOrigins.com sells a wide range of microgreen mixes and provides a wide range of tools for new growers. This site is a good option when you want to quality seeds that produce great results. It is also nice because it does offer the microgreens combinations - that makes it simple for you to create an even growing process.

CropKing.com offers a unique growing solution for those who want to grow microgreens. Check out the CropKing Microgreen System. This system makes it very easy to have everything you need to grow these crops quickly and without a lot of effort. You can grow as many as you would like to with this system, too. For those who want to grow more, this is the route to take.

In addition to these resources, you can find many of the products and materials you need online through many organic growers' websites. Your local gardening supply store will also provide you with the materials you need.

Videos

Here are a few videos that can provide you with the help you need to grow in your garden. If you are ready to transform your garden into a microgreen bed, these tips will help with some of the most common problems:

Tips for Using Clay Soil in an Organic Garden - http://video.about.com/organicgardening/Tips-for-Using-Clay-Soil-in-an-Organic-Garden.htm

Tips for Organic Container Gardening - http://video.about.com/organicgardening/Tips-for-Organic-Container-Gardening.htm

How to Grow Wheatgrass and Microgreens with the Sure To Grow Pad - http://www.youtube.com/watch?v=RsgXEtHMZTk
The Sure To Grow pad is a fantastic tool that can speed up the growing process and make the process even faster.

Westhaven Farm -Growing Microgreens - http://www.youtube.com/watch?v=JA8p5IT91H8
Check out the process of growing on a large scale as well as how these growers do such a fantastic job at the process. This is a good example of what you can grow if you would like to do so.

Growing microgreens is a fantastic way to boost your health, get your gardening skills going and to see significant improvement in the way you feel. Take the time to check out the resources provided here, but do take the first step. That step is simply to take the time to start growing. Pick up some seeds. Get them started. Moreover, watch as you can now add so much nutrition and flavor to your favorite dishes. The process is very easy and it can provide you with something to be very proud of. The good news is that it is not even that hard to pull off!

Growing microgreens is a great way to get your family involved, too. If you are looking for a way to add flavor, something pretty to a plate or just some added nutrition to your meals, this is the route to take.

Made in the USA
Monee, IL
06 January 2023

24620576R00026